Life Is
HARD

Life Is HARD

Answers for the Hard Places in Life

Donald Lunsford

Trilogy Christian Publishers

A Wholly Owned Subsidiary of Trinity Broadcasting Network

2442 Michelle Drive

Tustin, CA 92780

Copyright © 2024 by Donald Lunsford

Unless otherwise noted, Scripture quotations are taken from the Holy Bible, New International Version®, NIV®. Copyright © 1973, 1978, 1984, 2011 by Biblica, Inc.TM Used by permission of Zondervan. All rights reserved worldwide. www.zondervan.com. The "NIV" and "New International Version" are trademarks registered in the United States Patent and Trademark Office by Biblica, Inc.TM

Scripture quotations marked nkjv are taken from the New King James Version®. Copyright © 1982 by Thomas Nelson. Used by permission. All rights reserved.

All rights reserved, including the right to reproduce this book or portions thereof in any form whatsoever.

For information, address Trilogy Christian Publishing

Rights Department, 2442 Michelle Drive, Tustin, CA 92780.

Trilogy Christian Publishing/ TBN and colophon are trademarks of Trinity Broadcasting Network.

For information about special discounts for bulk purchases, please contact Trilogy Christian Publishing.

Trilogy Disclaimer: The views and content expressed in this book are those of the author and may not necessarily reflect the views and doctrine of Trilogy Christian Publishing or the Trinity Broadcasting Network.

10 9 8 7 6 5 4 3 2 1

Library of Congress Cataloging-in-Publication Data is available.

ISBN 979-8-89333-878-2

ISBN (ebook) 979-8-89333-879-9

Foreword

Pastor Joe Peterson, Christ Church, Palm Harbor, FL

What an honor to introduce you to Pastor Don Lunsford in this very needed and informative book. I have personally known Don Lunsford since the early 1970's. He has a rich heritage in ministry that has given him a wealth of knowledge and insight of human behavior. His experience in dealing with many people and their behavior in his successful pastorates, Assemblies of God leadership positions, assistant superintendent, and as a district superintendent, qualifies him to address these subjects in his book, *Life Is Hard, Answers for the Hard Places in Life*. The knowledge you will receive from the subjects in each chapter will help you to understand and give you the tools to confront and deal with the hard things in life.

I believe as you read this book it will help you develop Christian character, and you will be a better and stronger Christian. Once you begin reading you won't want to stop. Thank you, Don, for sharing your experiences and wisdom with each reader. I highly recommend this Biblical book that is going to be life changing for many people.

It's Hard to Forget

It's hard to forget when you have been wronged, mistreated, or judged. When someone takes it out on you, those incidents stick with you, and you want to avoid those situations in the future. So, you just avoid those people or companies you feel have stuck it to you. How do you forget it and move on?

If it is an individual that has offended you, you can't keep harboring the incident in your mind. Even though it's hard, you must forget it and move on. Otherwise, you will be emotionally crippled by the incident for the rest of your life. Forgiveness is not weakness; it's a sign of strength and freedom.

I've known people who have grown old and can still tell you about the offenses or abuses they received in their youth. The memories are stuck, and they cannot get over them.

In Cleveland, Ohio the evangelist met a lady wanting to accept Jesus Christ as her Savior. She was having difficulty in surrendering completely to Christ. Dr. Torrey looked at her and asked, "Is there somebody you cannot forgive?"

She quickly asked, "Who told you?"

Dr. Torrey said, "Nobody told me, and I have never seen you before tonight." Dr. Torrey questioned, "Has someone wronged or disappointed you and because of that injury, you will not come to Christ because you want to cherish this bitter grudge in your heart?" Revival addresses, R.A. Torrey.

Jesus is the greatest example of a forgiving spirit. When Peter, in anger, took out the sword and cut off the ear of the soldier who came to arrest Jesus, Jesus at once healed the severed ear. Even though He was innocent of the charges brought against Him causing the arrest, His healing of the severed ear shows a gracious, forgiving spirit. The incident was a rebuke to Peter, who acted out of his desire to protect Jesus. All indications are that Peter put behind him the rebuke; however, at the arrest and hearing Peter found a fire in the courtyard and was warming himself along with some of those in the crowd that arrested Jesus. One pointed his finger at Peter and said, "He is one of them!"

Peter cursed and said, "I don't know him." The rooster crowed, reminding him of the words of Jesus at the last supper, "Before the rooster crows you will deny me."

The principle of forgiveness is of great importance. Without it, we become enslaved to our pasts. With it, we become free in Christ. It is necessary to forgive those who have hurt us or wronged us; without forgiveness our wounds will fester and never heal.

The song says, "O to be like Him, o to be like Him, blessed redeemer, pure as thou art." To forget may require you to call on Jesus and ask Him to purify your memory and allow you to forget. That is better than a psychologist, and it costs nothing but faith to believe that He is the Great Physician. Jesus will heal the mind and emotions of hurt and pain and enable you to put it behind you.

Paul wrote to the Philippians, "Brethren, I do not count myself to have apprehended; but one thing I do, forgetting those things which are behind and reaching forward to those things which are ahead, I press toward the goal for the prize of the upward call of God in Christ Jesus" (Philippians 3:13,14).

It's Hard to Apologize

It's hard to apologize. To apologize means to express regret for something you have done. What makes it hard is that our self-defense mode kicks in and even though we have done wrong we find it hard to confess it, especially to someone who was affected by the action. Or, if in a public setting, to face the embarrassment of confessing a wrong action.

We are all guilty of saying or doing something that we should apologize for. I've been in this arena many times. I have spoken apologies, and written apologies. We are imperfect human beings. We all make mistakes. But some find it too hard to admit they were wrong. To apologize is to set aside pride and admit imperfections.

Why do we use our tongues so carelessly? Why are we so insensitive to others? What motivates us? If I had to guess, I would guess that most of our inhumanity to others is rooted in our own insecurities and sense of inadequacy. Like chickens fighting for a pecking order in the chicken coop, we fight each other for positions in the pecking order of humanity, often with words.

We have between our teeth a tool that gives us the ability to encourage, exalt, and empower, or the ability to discourage, damage, and defeat.

I've had some gracious people track me down to apologize for something they have said or done. That gave me great admiration for those who volunteered to make their apologies. Others have resisted apologizing for their misconduct or words. Those people I must pray for and forget the offense.

An apology is somewhat like repentance. To apologize, you must recognize the wrong you have done. "For all have sinned and fall short of the glory of God" (Romans 3:23). We must admit our failures and shortcomings. So, apologize to God and repent of your sins.

We are often owed an apology and may unconsciously owe an apology. Only the grace of God can heal the wounds of our experiences. As I said in the "It's Hard to Forget," when we are owed an apology, it may never come, so forget it and move ahead!

Back in the days when local grocery stores sold groceries on credit, a grocery store owner became worried about an accumulation of accounts past due from people that had apparently ceased buying. The accountant sent all of them a bill for more than double the amount they owed. The plan proved unusually successful. People who paid no attention to the correct bills wrote, telephoned, or came in person to demand an explanation, giving the accountant an opportunity to apologize for the "mistake," and at the same time to remind the debtor it was past time he paid something on the account.

It's Hard to Save Money

It's hard to save money; human nature is to want it and want it now! That kind of action would often require you to borrow money, or use the credit card, which is the same as borrowing money; you must pay it back at a higher cost than the original price due to the interest on the loan. Be mindful of lifestyle creep and prioritize saving over unnecessary spending.

Some things are necessities, such as buying or renting a home, or buying an automobile that will usually require borrowing or financing. Buying food and clothing is necessary. In our modern age buying electricity and paying for the internet is essential to our livelihood. So, now the question is, how do we manage it all? Practice mindful spending and avoid impulsive purchases.

Managing it all is the reason it is hard to save money, yet saving is essential to living well in our later years. We cannot always live our lives in the NOW; the future is on the way.

Much of my life's work has required a lot of travel, not only by air, but also by automobile. I've put over one hundred thousand on a few automobiles. That means that I had to resist the latest styles that seem at times irresistible, which requires self-control. The big spender and impulse buyer do not have their eyes on the future; they are living in the now.

Here is a formula for preparing for your future.

Begin saving as early in life as possible. If your job provides a 401K or a non-profit 403B, sign up for it. Some companies only provide retirement investment in their company.

My recommendation would be a mutual fund that invests in dividend-paying companies, and then request that dividends be reinvested into the fund. The earlier you do this, the better retirement you can expect. When every dollar is allocated, saving becomes challenging.

My policy, since I'm not rich, is to only invest in well-managed companies whose shares are under $55 per share and pay dividends. There are many good companies that match that criterion, although as the market is rising, it's getting more difficult to find companies with that low share price. I've broken that $55 rule a couple of times when I discovered a stock that was just too tempting. Mutual funds are usually well managed, and because of their volume can buy the more expensive stocks. Mutual funds allow you to own a piece of companies that you could not afford on your own.

Credit cards: credit cards are good for paying for goods and services; however, they carry a very high amount of interest. No matter what interest they charge, if you pay the full amount each month you will pay no interest. If you pay only the minimum, the interest amount will increase month to month until you're in too deep to get out. Many credit cards charge no annual fee.

Decide to give to God through your church what He requires. Here are Apostle Paul's directions on giving. "Remember this: Whoever sows sparingly will also reap sparingly, and whoever sows generously will also reap generously. Each of you should give what you have decided in your heart to give, not reluctantly or under compulsion, for God loves a cheerful giver" (2 Corinthians 9:6, 7).

Give yourself at least ten percent of your earnings to investments, savings, and retirement funds.

23 The Lord makes firm the steps of the one who delights in him; 24 though he may stumble, he will not fall, for the Lord upholds him with his hand. 25 I was young and now I am old, yet I have never seen the righteous forsaken or their children begging for bread (Psalms 37 NIV).

There is a qualifier for this passage; it is verse 23, "The steps of a good man are ordered by the Lord, and He delights in his way" (NKJV). The "good" in this verse means that this man or woman is serving the Lord and following in the path where He leads. Success in the meeting of our needs is that we follow in His way. The stewardship of our lives requires it. Don't forget what the Apostle Paul has to say about our giving responsibility. "6 Remember this: Whoever sows sparingly will also reap sparingly, and whoever sows generously will also reap generously. 7 Each of you should give what you have decided in your heart to give, not reluctantly or under compulsion, for God loves a cheerful giver" (2 Corinthians 9:6, 7).

It's Hard to Be Unselfish

It's hard to be unselfish. Selfishness is born in us. Just watch babies playing together; whether a visiting baby or a sibling, they protect their toys. They will fight and scream if one takes the other's toy. That is human nature showing itself. We just don't like to share. In adults, you could call it greed. We want what someone else has, and the evil person will steal it. We see it in the cities, gangs breaking into stores to steal the products. Their attitude is the store has plenty and doesn't need to make the profit from it, so we are justified in stealing it. That is the evil that surrounds us today. These actions around us make it difficult to be unselfish. Selfishness can significantly impact our behavior and interactions with others.

How do we know the man on the street holding up a sign "will work for food" is legitimate?

I have often stopped to tell them I have work at the church, and I will take them to a restaurant, before work or after. Invariably, they would ask, "What kind of work?"

When I told them their reply would be, "I can't do that" for one reason or another. Their sign was to play on sympathy. Many people would respond by just giving them money. After many refusals, I stopped asking them to do the work.

As a pastor I have often set up an account at a restaurant to direct people who were hungry to go to and the restaurant would feed those I sent, and I would later come by the restaurant and pay the bill. I have many stories I could tell, but one stands out to me at this moment. I had an account at a Denny's restaurant near the church. Late one evening I received

Donald Lunsford

from the restaurant manager who asked me, "Did you send two men named ------to get food?"

My answer was, "No, I have not met those men and did not send them."

The manager said, "I'm going to fill their order anyway; I knew they were not legitimate, sorry to bother you with the call. After I feed them, I will present them with the bill. If they do not pay, I'll tell them that I plan to report them to the authorities." The next morning, I stopped by Denny's to ask about the outcome of the incident. The manager on duty told me that when they were confronted with the bill and told the consequences they paid and walked out. They had ordered the most expensive cut of steak, and their bill was not small. Such is greed and looking to take advantage of every opportunity.

Two of Jesus' disciples, James and John, asked to be given positions of honor when Jesus established His kingdom. The other ten disciples resented their request and complained about it. So, Jesus called them together to solve the dispute.

Jesus called them together and said, "You know that those who are regarded as rulers of the Gentiles lord it over them, and their high officials exercise authority over them. Not so with you. Instead, whoever wants to become great among you must be your servant, and whoever wants to be first must be slave of all. For even the Son of Man did not come to be served, but to serve, and to give his life as a ransom for many" (Mark 10:42-45).

Not only did Jesus teach this, He lived it. He washed His own disciples' grimy feet, a chore normally reserved for a slave. See John 2:1-4.

Obviously, we cannot meet everyone's needs. Jesus Himself admitted that the poor would always be with us. If we gave away all our money, we would not make a dent in poverty, and our own families would be in poverty. If we spent one hundred percent serving others, we would soon be exhausted. Jesus rested and enjoyed time for Himself.

Nevertheless, we should help others in need when it is within our power to do so.

"Do nothing out of selfish ambition or vain conceit. Rather, in humility value others above yourselves, not looking to your own interests but each of you to the interests of the others" (Philippians 2:3-4). This passage does not mean that we are to be taken advantage of by those who have selfish motives. To quote former president Ronald Reagan, "Trust, but verify."

It's Hard to Avoid Mistakes

It's hard to avoid mistakes. Theodore Roosevelt said, "Show me a man who makes no mistakes, and I will show you a man who doesn't do things."

A ship passenger reported that his clothes were gone. The steward asked, "Where did you put them?"

The passenger replied, "In that little cupboard with the glass door."

The steward answered, "Bless me, that's no cupboard – that's a porthole, sir."

When a plumber makes a mistake, he charges for it.

When a lawyer makes a mistake, it is just what he wanted, because he has a chance to try the case again.

When a carpenter makes a mistake, it must be corrected, because the fittings won't work.

When a doctor makes a mistake, he buries it.

When a judge makes a mistake, it becomes the law of the land.

But when an editor makes a mistake, they just overlook it.

Experience is a wonderful thing. It enables you to recognize a mistake when you make it again.

I don't have any Scripture to help with mistakes, oth

Donald Lunsfor

the mistake of ignoring God's plan of salvation that cleanses from all sin brought on by the mistake made by Adam and Eve in the Garden of Eden. This was their disobedience which caused the sin nature to pass to all humankind.

The remedy for that mistake is the sacrifice of Jesus Christ on the cross of Calvary.

"For God so loved the world that he gave his one and only Son, that whoever believes in him shall not perish but have eternal life" (John 3:16 NIV).

It's Hard to Keep Out Of A Rut

It's hard to keep out of a rut. J. C. Penney said, "The best way to stop a bad habit is never to begin it."

When I was a small boy, I was given a cucumber in a small necked bottle. The cucumber was large enough to fill up the bottle. The question was, how did they get that cucumber into the bottle? There was no sign that the bottom had been cut out and glued back. I was puzzled. Then one day visiting the second cousin that had given me the cucumber in the bottle, I saw in the garden a bottle slipped over a little green pickle looking like it might become a cucumber. Then I understood. The cucumber had grown in the bottle.

When I see people with habits – in a rut they seem unable to get out of—then I realize that it did not happen suddenly. Very likely they grew into them, maybe when they were young, and now cannot slip out of them. They are like the cucumber in the bottle!

The greatest rut is drug or alcohol addiction.

A man named Smith was generally a source of irritation to his wife and family at home. His wife attributed his irritably to his excessive use of alcohol, but the husband insisted that that was not the source of his difficulties and refused to listen to her counsel that he abstain from his drinking. She finally persuaded him to see his doctor. He made an appointment with his doctor. After the doctor's examination he told him, much to his chagrin, just what his wife had told him. The doctor that his excessive use of alcohol was responsible for all his difficulties and told him if he hoped for relief, he would have to stop the alcohol use.

Upon leaving the doctor's office, Smith was terribly upset. He hated to go home and to admit to his wife that she was right. That would merely make things even less tolerable for him. As he made his way homeward, he kept trying to think of something he would be able to tell his wife without having to admit the truth. Then he looked up and saw a sign at the front entrance of a music hall. "Syncopation," and thought he had found the answer to his problem. On his arrival home, his wife inquired of him what the doctor had diagnosed. He answered, "The doctor says I have 'syncopation,' my dear."

"Syncopation!" she said. "What's that?"

"Well, I don't know how to tell you, but the best thing for you to do is look it up in the dictionary."

His wife did—and there it was: "Syncopation—Intermittent progress from bar to bar."

Here are some questions to ask yourself:

What are some of the things that consistently build up to become big things in your life?

What can you do to begin correcting the little irritations in your life?

Do you have trouble dealing with guilt over your failures?

What can you do to turn an irritation into an opportunity?

What does the Bible say about getting out of the rut? "You were taught, with regard to your former life, to put off your old self, which is being corrupted by its deceitful desires; to be made new in the attitude of your minds; and put on the new self, created to be like God in true righteousness and holiness" (Ephesians 4:22-24).

Donald Lunsfo

It's Hard to Make A New Start

It's hard to make a new start. Some incidents in life create situations that require a new start. Loss of a job, a divorce, remarriage, a crippling accident, the list goes on.

Finding a new employer in a job you are suited and trained for may not be easily accomplished. The search is often disappointing and exhausting. It can result in a lack of confidence in yourself.

A divorce is grievous, sorting the results of dealing with who gets the children, where the divorcee or divorced will live, how they will make a living. The anger that brought about the divorce may still linger. The blame game is in play. A new start is necessary.

From the Louisville Courier Journal, "There is entirely too much worrying about unhappy marriages. All marriages are happy. It's only living together afterward that causes the trouble."

After the loss of a mate, remarriage too often results in the same mistakes that caused the disruption in the first marriage.

A new start may require some character adjustments. Most of the time humanity is unable to make the changes necessary to be successful in a new start. Some consult counselors, others try to do it on their own. Life is dynamic, and adaptability is essential for growth and resilience.

Remember, every fresh start is an opportunity to shape your future. Approach it with curiosity, courage, and a willing-

Donald Lunsford

ness to learn!

Only God can bring about a new full start.

"Therefore, if anyone is in Christ, he is a new creation; old things have passed away; behold, all things have become new" (2 Corinthians 5:17 NKJV).

Place your trust in God and He will direct your steps in your new start.

It's Hard to Make The Best Of Things

Some things cannot be changed. Thinking "I wish things were different" won't change anything. We must try to make the best of things that cannot be changed. No matter how hard we try to always make our lives work, things do go wrong. Life is filled with disasters, and things can look bleak even when we think we've done everything right. Bad things happen, but it's up to us to choose how we respond.

The situations we experience in life are a chance to learn and grow. However, sometimes it is hard to see the opportunity due to the layers of emotion we build up around ourselves. We know people that have made it through dark times and have come through them successfully. Going through a disastrous time yourself is different; it can feel like there's no way out.

Not everything that happens to us is good. But God will use everything for good. What is accumulating in your life? Is it the endless drudgery of administrative details you have to address because there is no delegate to resolve it? The frustration of dealing with a teenager whom you don't understand and who doesn't seem to understand you? Is it the frustration of working endlessly and yet not making enough money to make ends meet?

In life things do go wrong, and we must choose how to respond. Seek God for His help in responding to these disappointments.

At some point in life, we will deal with grief. At that time, we must face the loss. It does no good to linger in grief. You must accept what you cannot change. Be honest about the pain you feel and recognize that life goes on. Life is hard, there's no question about it, but you must be tougher! The Apostle Paul wrote, "I can do all things through Christ who strengthens me" (Philippians 4:13).

The difference between those who make it and those who don't is not some mystical trick or advanced genetic advantage. Those who truly succeed in life choose the genuine way of life. It is easy to get caught up in bad things that happen to us. But there is a path to take that can lead in the right direction.

Psalms 37:23-24 comes to mind again. "The Lord makes firm the steps of the one who delights in him; though he may stumble, he will not fall, for the Lord upholds him with his hand."

Yes, I have experienced those dark times when there seems to be no way out. Yet, my dependence on God and following His way led me out of the dark times and into glorious light and success. Jesus' words to Peter were "Follow Me..." Peter's answer to the call made him a great apostle whose writings, through the centuries, have brought the overcoming truth to millions across the ages. I have followed the path that God laid out for me, and He has delivered me out of the dark places and into victorious outcomes.

Jesus teaches His followers to trust God to provide for their needs. He tells them to seek God's kingdom and His righteousness, which means living in the ways of Jesus and following His commands. "But seek first his kingdom and his righteousness, and all these things will be given to you as well" (Matthew 6:33). He promises that if they do so, all the things they need will be given to them.

This is not just "pie in the sky," it is the pattern for a successful life.

It's Hard to Hold Your Temper

Situations that suddenly present themselves make it hard to keep your temper in check.

"He who can suppress a moment's anger may prevent a day of sorrow." -- Tryon Edwards

Do you fume when someone cuts you off in traffic? Does your blood pressure rocket when your child refuses to cooperate? Anger is a common and even healthy emotion. But it's important to deal with it in a positive way. Uncontrolled anger can take a toll on both your health and your relationships.

In the heat of the moment, it's easy to say something you'll later regret. Take a few moments to collect your thoughts before saying anything. Practice thinking before you speak, even if it takes counting to ten before you reply.

As soon as you're thinking clearly, express your frustration in a non-confrontational way. State your concerns and needs clearly and directly, without hurting others or trying to control them.

Instead of focusing on what made you mad, work on resolving the issue at hand. Does your child's messy room make you upset? Close the door. Is your partner late for dinner every night? Schedule meals later in the evening. Or agree to eat on your own a few times a week. Also, understand that some things are simply out of your control. Try to be realistic about what you can and cannot change. Remind yourself that anger won't fix anything and might only make it worse.

Forgiveness is a powerful tool. If you allow anger and other negative feelings to crowd out positive feelings, you might find yourself swallowed up by your own bitterness or sense of injustice. Forgiving someone who angered you might help you both learn from the situation and strengthen your relationship.

What does the Bible have to say about temper, anger, and self-control?

(Ephesians 4:29 NKJV) "Let no corrupt word proceed out of your mouth, but what is good for necessary edification, that it may impart grace to the hearers."

(Ephesians 26-27) "'In your anger do not sin:" Do not let the sun go down while you are still angry, and do not give the devil a foothold."

(James 1:19-20) "My dear brothers and sisters, take note of this: Everyone should be quick to listen, slow to speak and slow to become angry, because human anger does not produce the righteousness that God desires."

It's Hard to Keep A High Standard

The hardest high standard to keep is the spiritual high standard. There are so many interferences that creep into our daily routines that make it hard to find time to pray, go to church, and practice the standards of spiritual victory to which we strive.

Priorities matter! To maintain the high standard, we must set and maintain priorities. Whatever our priorities are, they will take control of our life. If sports events are a priority of our time and activity, they have the upper hand. If work schedules interfere with our church attendance and prayer life, our work has the priority. I will admit that we must work to make a living, but we must find a way to not allow our work to overpower our Christian responsibilities. We must make time for the service of our Lord.

Every person is building a track record. The track record is in relationships, in employment, and in serving Christ. That track record can be a good one, an average one, or a poor one. What we did yesterday we will probably tend to do tomorrow; current performance is vital in assessing future performance. I'm not saying that a person can never change. I know I have changed and would be disappointed if people judged me today on the basis of my performance in the past.

My mother saved all my report cards from first grade through high school. When I married and had children, Mom gave me all the report cards she had saved. I looked them over and was reminded of how little effort I put into my education, not only the grades, although I did pass every class, I was also disappointed with the grades of my deportment. I told Mom, "You should have trashed these reports years ago. I'm going to trash them now." I certainly hold myself to a higher standard now.

The only way to overcome a poor track record is to prove that you have broken the old patterns and replaced them with good ones.

The Apostle Paul wrote, "I press on toward the goal to win the prize for which God has call me heavenward in Christ Jesus, forgetting what is behind and straining toward what is ahead" (Philippians 3:14).

Yes, to keep on keeping on requires the effort of "straining" toward the goal. As the title of this book says, *Life Is Hard!* A disordered life can and should be rearranged and made harmonious. Do not repress the Holy Spirit's directives; they will lead you in the paths of righteousness.

It's Hard to Keep Out The Trash

One of my household jobs is taking out the trash. Even though our trash is picked up twice weekly, the bag is often heavy to carry to the street for pickup. Either we are the cleanest people on the block or the most wasteful.

Have you ever seen pictures of large cities where there has been a union strike for trash pickup? The streets become piled with trash of all sorts until the sidewalks are almost impassable, and the rats are running everywhere.

Now think about your mind. If it is continually filled with trash and your spiritual life is on strike, the trash will eventually fill your mind, and "a mind is a terrible thing to waste."

The heart is often used in the Bible to describe the mind. That makes the heart the center of our being. You are still considered alive until the heart stops beating. The Bible speaks of the heart and the mind and usually when it says "heart" it is speaking about the center of our being. It is the mind that determines our behavior, and our behavior cannot be changed without a transformation. Without that inward change, an encounter with God, we cannot follow God's plan. "For out of the abundance of the heart (mind) his mouth speaks" (Matthew 12:34 and Luke 6:45).

Our language can reveal the condition of our mental state. It can also reveal our spiritual condition.

A rich man had sent his son so that Socrates might look

him over and judge of his talents. "Well, then, my lad," said Socrates, "speak, so that I can see you." We often quote that statement as "speak that I may know you."

In the 15th century, Erasmus said: "…meaning thereby that a man's character is reflected less fully in his face than in his speech."

Be careful what you store in your brain. If we put worthless, inaccurate, or faulty information into our minds, that is all we will get out of it. There is an old computer term, GIGO, which is garbage in/garbage out. It means if you put worthless inaccurate, or faulty information into a computer, you will get worthless, inaccurate, or faulty information out of it.

"For as he thinks in his heart, so is he" (Proverbs 23:7). The mind is occupied by what is put into it and what it dwells upon. It is amazing how like a computer the mind is. The computer has a large memory bank where it stores whatever you put into it.

We are now in the internet world coping with AI, Artificial Intelligence. As I wrote this line, as soon as I put in the initial AI, immediately my word processor wrote Artificial Intelligence.

Like AI on computers, the mind can create its own worthless, inaccurate, or faulty information. It does not have to come from the outside. That is why it is so critical that we exercise great care in what we allow into our mind and what we allow our mind to dwell on.

Trouble places in our thought life.

The media is probably the most powerful influence the mind has ever encountered. Television, movies, magazines, and music embed powerful images, thoughts, and values. They often settle deeply into our minds. They either help us or hurt us.

The reason there is so much violence today is because the youth of today are filling their minds with violent content. The heroes in the games kill, wreck, and destroy. The care with which we guard what is allowed into our minds is crucial to our ability to know and do the will of God.

Be careful about the company you keep. Do not be misled: "Bad company corrupts good character" (1 Corinthians 15:33). The company we keep influences our mental attitudes and becomes trash in the brain. There is no trash pickup for the trash in our brain. That requires a different cleansing agent.

Don't allow yourself to be double-minded. We must determine in our minds what we will believe, what we will let in, and what we will keep out. That determines how we will live. Our friends also have a dramatic impact on our values and behavior. "Bad company corrupts good character."

If you are not decided in your mind who you are and hang out with a foulmouthed crowd, it fills your mind with garbage. It will eventually cause the revelation of your state of mind, because "From the abundance of the heart the mouth speaks."

We must speak truthfully without using profane, obscene, or rude language. I think I may have heard this phrase, not spoken to me, but in my hearing. "You mind your language, young man, or you'll be grounded for the weekend!"

I was watching a young mother being interviewed on TV and she said, "We have been trying to mind our language around the kids. They're at the age now where they'll start repeating everything we say!"

How do we purify our minds? Paul gives the answer. "Do not conform to the pattern of this world but be transformed by the renewing of your mind. Then you will be able to test and approve what God's will is—his good, pleasing and perfect will" (Romans 12:2).

How do we renew our minds? By stopping the inflow of hurtful input and increasing the flow of helpful input. We must input positive data that will give victory over our worldly minds. We must pursue spiritual disciplines, such as prayer, Bible reading and Bible study, church attendance, and choosing to hang with friends who are living right, or righteously. We become what influences us and what we think.

Focus on right thoughts. "Finally, brothers and sisters, whatever is true, whatever is noble, whatever is right, whatever is pure, whatever is lovely, whatever is admirable—if anything is excellent or praiseworthy—think about such things. Whatever you have learned or received or heard from me or seen in me—put it into practice. And the God of peace will be with you" (Philippians 4:8-9).

People who are caught in the bondage of deeply ingrained habits find it very hard to break the deeply ingrained practices. If you are in the habit of cursing, or using "like" or "you know," that is unnecessary speech punctuation; the habit is difficult to break.

Unnecessary speech punctuation is a phrase I made up to describe speech that is laced with unnecessary words. These are vulgar, cursing, or unnecessary words that many use in their speech that add nothing to the sentence. Some people cannot even carry on a conversation without lacing their sentences with USP.

Whether it is lust, materialism, anger, resentment, fear, anxiety, worry, or anything else, garbage in will yield garbage out. If we feed our minds with ungodly information, we will make the wrong decisions, have wrong values, trust the wrong things, and we will suffer badly for it all. We become what we think about!

"Let no corrupt word proceed out of your mouth, but what

is good for necessary edification, that it may impart grace to the hearers" (Ephesians 4:29 NKJV).

And the peace of God, which transcends all understanding, will guard your hearts and your minds in Christ Jesus. Finally, brothers and sisters, whatever is true, whatever is noble, whatever is right, whatever is pure, whatever is lovely, whatever is admirable—if anything is excellent or praiseworthy—think about such things. Whatever you have learned or received or heard from me or seen in me—put it into practice. And the God of peace will be with you (Philippians 4:7-9).

It's Hard to Shoulder The Blame

It's always someone else's fault. We don't really have to try very hard to find someone to blame.

A collector of historic paintings had one of the Leaning Tower of Pisa on the wall behind his desk. He was disturbed and curious because he found himself straightening it every morning. Each morning, he found the painting hanging crooked. After a few mornings of straightening the painting, he asked the cleaning lady about the incidents. The cleaning lady explained: "I must hang it crooked to make the tower hangs straight."

Some people find it necessary to twist the story to justify and make their own actions appear right.

"The greatest of faults is to be conscious of none." - Thomas Carlyle

"Nothing is easier than fault-finding; no talent, no self-denial, no brains, no character are required to set up in the grumbling business." - Robert West

It's Hard to Admit Error

> A man who has committed a mistake and doesn't correct it is committing another mistake. - Confucius

A hard phrase is, "Sorry, I committed an error." No one is perfect; we have all committed errors and made mistakes.

While I was in grade school, I struggled with grammar. My grammarian errors were too many to list. It is good that I married a girl who was well schooled in grammar. I often had her edit my notes and writing. My young Ozark speech was well ingrained. My preaching beginnings were in the Ozarks, so, my English language fit their way of speaking. Over the years I have become more proficient in the English language.

While ministering a few days in the Lisbon, Portugal Bible College chapel, I was teamed with a Bible professor from Great Brittain. He did not hesitate to correct me personally on my grammar. I would just brush him off by saying, "I'm leaving it to my interpreter to put it correctly into Portuguese." The Brit was not my interpreter. I told the Brit, "Your car has a bonnet, mine has a hood. Your car has boot, mine has a trunk. See, our English language is different."

If a mistake or error has affected someone negatively, the responsibility of correcting the error lies with the one who caused it. If it is a financial error, the one who made it must make the correction. If it is an error of misrepresentation, admit it and correct it. Yes, it is hard to do and especially if the one affected is a long way off.

We live in an era of misrepresentations. People in politics are the ones most often who are making misrepresentations. So many politicos' think that Americans are not smart enough to know the things that are being misrepresented. Too often we accept what is said as truth, and never verify if it is truth.

It's Hard to Take Advice

Accepting advice is an essential skill that involves both openness and self-awareness. If you find it challenging to accept volunteered advice, reflect on your resistance and take a moment to understand why. Self-reflection can help you identify any emotional barriers or biases that might be getting in the way. We should view advice as an opportunity rather than a threat. Recognize that accepting help is not a sign of weakness but a way to enrich relationships and grow personally. Put yourself in the adviser's shoes. Consider their intentions and perspective.

Learn from others: realize that advice is not just about consuming wisdom; it's a practical skill that can be developed.

Seek out advice intentionally and learn from the experiences of others: when I was pastoring a growing church, I sought advice from those whom I knew had large, growing churches. One had written articles on matters where I needed advice. He would say, "My article or book will be coming to you in the mail."

When seeking an adviser: find the right fit; choose advisers whose insights resonate with you. Ensure both parties understand the context and problem.

Remember, accepting advice is not passive—it's an active process that involves growth, learning, and openness.

It's Hard to Forgive

Who hasn't been hurt by the actions or words of another? Letting go of grudges and bitterness involves an intentional decision to release resentment and anger. The act that hurt or offended you might always be with you. But working on forgiveness can lessen that act's grip on your emotional health. Maybe you've had a traumatic experience, such as being physically or emotionally abused by someone close to you. These wounds can leave lasting feelings of resentment, bitterness, and anger — sometimes even hatred.

Jesus preached forgiveness and, on the cross, modeled it. Three felons were crucified at Golgotha. One of the criminals who hung there hurled insults at him: "Aren't you the Messiah? Save yourself and us!" 40 But the other criminal rebuked him. "Don't you fear God," he said, "since you are under the same sentence? 41 We are punished justly, for we are getting what our deeds deserve. But this man has done nothing wrong." 42 Then he said, "Jesus, remember me when you come into your kingdom." 43 Jesus answered him, "Truly I tell you, today you will be with me in paradise." As we see in Luke 23:39-43, the last act of Christ on the cross was to forgive a convicted felon and promise a place in paradise for him.

Forgiveness can stop the cycle of hurt and pain, bringing us real peace. By embracing forgiveness, you can also embrace peace and hope. Consider how forgiveness can lead you down the path of physical, emotional, and spiritual well-being.

Forgiveness doesn't mean forgetting or excusing the harm done to you. It also doesn't necessarily mean making up with the person who caused the harm. Forgiveness brings a kind of peace that allows you to focus on yourself and helps you go on with life.

What if the person I'm forgiving doesn't change?

Getting another person to change isn't the point of forgiveness. It's about focusing on what you can control in yourself. Think of forgiveness as more about how it can change your life by bringing you peace, happiness, and emotional and spiritual healing. Forgiveness can take away the power of the other person that continues to have a grip in your life.

Even when rejecting hatred and resentment was hard, Jesus chose forgiveness. He offered that forgiveness freely, and His call is for us to do the same. These are all things the Holy Spirit inspires and enables us to do.

"Therefore, if you are offering your gift at the altar and there remember that your brother or sister has something against you, leave your gift there in front of the altar. First go and be reconciled to them; then come and offer your gift" (Matthew 5:23-24).

If we don't ask for forgiveness when we wrong someone, we lose our moral authority.

Finally

Finally, many of the answers I've given are from my lifetime experiences in ministry and counseling. Those, along with the teachings of the Bible, have formed these lifetime values. After living in the service of our Lord for many years, I look back on my life and realize the paths I've traveled have been led by the directives of the Holy Spirit. They were good paths, not always smooth, yet in the end, good. I hope you will find answers for your life in these pages.

I trust that the advice I've given in this book will be a guiding light for your life and you can look back and say, "I have no regrets."

Milton Keynes UK
Ingram Content Group UK Ltd.
UKHW031618231124
451036UK00003B/26